Welcome to the Offi [illegible] of

MIB

MEN IN BLACK™
THE SERIES

This fun-filled, action-packed animated adventure series explores the possibility that aliens live among us...and we don't even know it!

Designed by Traffika Publishing Limited

Published by
Grandreams Ltd
435-437 Edgware Road
Little Venice
London W2 1TH

Printed in Belgium

CONTENTS

The condensed stories in this annual are adapted from original Men in Black™: The Series scripts.

WHO ARE THE MEN IN BLACK™?

Aliens have been around for so long that there is actually a government team whose purpose it is to ensure that foreign beings follow rules and regulations. This organisation, better known as Men in Black (MiB), works tirelessly to 'protect the Earth from the scum of the universe'.

The MiB was organised in 1961, when the Immigration and Naturalisation Service of Aliens (INSA) discovered that human beings weren't the only intelligent life form in the galaxy.

They learned that a multitude of planets inhabited by other life forms exist beyond our solar system and, as fate would have it, Earth ranked as a 'five star' travel destination for some. After all, Mother Earth has top-notch resources, varied terrain and hundreds of species – making it a great place for vacation, research and, unfortunately, crime.

Intense negotiations took place between the Intergalactic Travel Commission and the INSA outlining the rules that aliens must obey in order to be granted admission to Earth.

The rules state that aliens on Earth must disguise themselves as humans or inanimate objects at all times, acknowledge the unquestioned authority of the MiB and refrain from engaging in criminal activity of any kind.

In exchange for granting the aliens habitation rights, human beings receive some pretty cool, previously undiscovered alien technology. (You didn't think that the CD-ROM and 'hip-hop' music were human inventions!!!) Hence, an intergalactic policing agency for alien beings was launched.

Being a member of the MiB is not a glamorous job. Once signed on, these agents must cut ties with their past completely, leaving all their friends, family and fingerprints behind. And since part of their job is to keep the existence of the alien beings a secret from the public, Earthlings never know and can't appreciate when or how often the Men in Black save lives...

MIB
MEN IN BLACK
THE SERIES

MEET THE MiB

KAY

A veteran MiB agent who's been around the block a few times and has seen things beyond the comprehension of most humans.

Kay's life is the MiB and he is fearless, but he sometimes loses touch with his humanity. To become a member of the MiB, he had to leave behind his high-school sweetheart, the love of his life, because for the MiB, leaving one's past behind is part of the job.

With an 'all-business' attitude, Kay is not one for making jokes. However, he does enjoy delivering a few wisecracks at Jay's expense.

AGENTS...

JAY

A rookie with the MiB. Jay is still learning the ropes and is constantly surprised by what he's up against.

A former NYPD cop who was recruited by Kay to be his partner, Jay is enthusiastic, comic and cool.

Being partnered by Kay is no picnic and Jay is determined to force Kay to crack a smile – no easy task. Sometimes Jay misses the life he once had, but he especially enjoys the intense action and awesome alien weaponry that are literally 'out of this world' – he really digs being in the MiB.

Being the newest kid on the block means Jay does all the dirty work and Kay personally sees to it that Jay gets no special treatment. In turn, Jay is continually cracking jokes at Kay's expense, keeping the boisterous banter between the two MiB agents at the forefront of their relationship.

ELLE

Truly a woman of the '90s, Elle is strong, brilliant and totally self-confident. She joined the MiB agency as a research assistant, but her goal is to one day become a fully-fledged agent.

By calling herself a 'field scientist', Elle is sometimes able to get close to the heart of the action – which is exactly where she wants to be! She's just as likely to be out and about New York taking samples of the remnants of an Uxmarian vapour trail, as she would be in the MiB Command Centre lab analysing DNA.

For the most part, it is Elle who the MiB agents turn to for any biochemical, physics-based or forensic information. And, if she can offer any useful information to the agents, she will.

ZED

Zed, the MiB's head honcho, runs the whole shebang from the MiB Command Centre. He juggles a million tasks at once while serving as the organisation's Commander-in-Chief and Number One agent.

Extremely intelligent and cunning, Zed tries to acquire as much information as possible from all of the alien races, including their languages, cultures and even their mind-reading techniques.

HOW THE MiB FOUND AN ALIEN AT THE MOVIES...

Kay and Jay kicked open the doors of the darkened movie theatre. Their torch beams cut through the darkness and swept across the audience.

A 'space aliens' movie was showing and the audience was gripped by a scene of an astronaut hiding from an horrific-looking alien in the murky engine room of his spacecraft.

Jay and Kay glanced around at the faces of the gasping audience.

'How are we supposed to find the perp in here?' Jay asked aloud. 'Place is packed.'

A huge '*Shhhhssssssh!*' rose from the audience.

'It's okay, we're ushers,' said Kay, turning to Jay and whispering, 'to catch an alien, you have to think like one. Ask yourself...why would an alien go to a horror movie about an alien...?'

On the screen the growling alien attacked the unfortunate astronaut who let out a bloodcurdling scream. The entire audience was horrified...Except for one man – who burst out *laughing*.

'...Because he thinks it's a comedy,' said Jay.

The Men in Black knew they had their alien.

They shoved their way past protesting cinema-goers and rushed the laughing 'man' – who transformed into a *real life* hideous alien!

The audience screamed as Jay wrestled the vile creature to the ground. Then Kay stepped up and slapped a huge pair of cuffs on him.

They slipped on their shades, and Kay held up a Neuralyser.

'Remember, folks, it's only a movie,' he said.

And the Neuralyser flashed, erasing the incident from the minds of everyone in the cinema.

THE PSYCHIC LINK SYNDROME

Based on the episode "The Psychic Link Syndrome" written by Steve Roberts
Based on the Malibu Comic by Lowell Cunningham

A wide-eyed tourist sat in the back of a yellow cab as it passed the Empire State Building. He pointed his camera up at the famous landmark, focused and snapped a picture.

'My first time in the Big Apple,' he said to the driver. 'I'm from Rickford, Illinois. Where you from?'

The cabbie glanced disapprovingly in his rear-view mirror, as if to say: 'Wouldn't you like to know?'

If the tourist had looked closer, he would have noticed that the cab driver's eyes were bright lime green.

As the cab screeched up to the front of the hotel, the tourist handed money to the driver. 'Keep the change,' he said, while grabbing a business card from inside the cab.

He hopped out and lifted the camera to his eye once again. 'Hold on. I wanna get a picture of a real New York cabbie.'

As the camera snapped, the driver shielded his face and recoiled as if in fear.

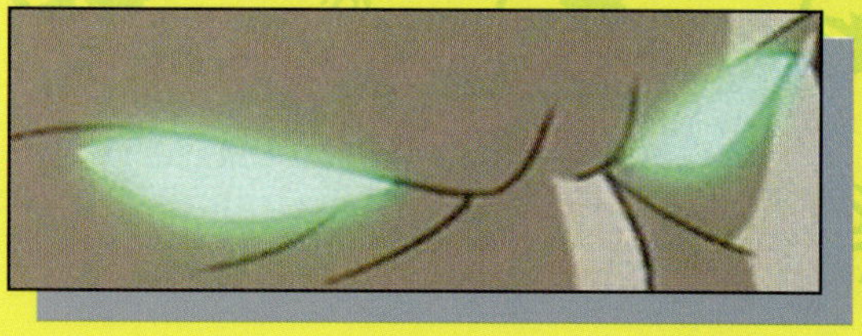

Inside the hotel, the tourist headed straight for the empty elevator and pressed a button. Just as the doors were closing, a hand shot in – followed by the cabbie.

'Hi, again...' said the tourist, as the doors closed.

The driver looked very, very angry – and the tourist was suddenly very, very scared.

'Did I undertip?' he asked, taking out his wallet and tossing it at the driver. 'Take it!'

But the silent and menacing driver just stood there.

'Wh-what do you want from me?' whimpered the tourist.

'Your *essence*,' answered the driver, morphing into his true alien form. He was Forbus, a hideous wild-eyed Alcidian.

He turned ominously towards the tourist, whose eyes widened while his mouth dropped in absolute terror.

Moments later, a man and a woman waited as the elevator doors opened and Forbus – in human form again – stepped out.

The woman looked down and screamed.

On the floor of the elevator lay the shrivelled and desiccated remains of the poor guy from Rickford, Illinois.

The MiB Clean-Up van whisked away the tourist before the ambulance arrived. As it sped back to headquarters, Elle used a high-tech diagnostic camera to examine the tourist while Kay and Jay looked on. The camera then produced all sorts of statistics.

'That is one ugly alien,' said Jay.

'Not an alien, Slick,' said Kay. 'He's a grade-A bona fide human, like you or me.'

''Cept he's missing most of his bodily fluids,' confirmed Elle, as she showed Jay the diagnostic photos.

Repulsed but fascinated, Jay bent to take a closer look.

Suddenly the tourist's hand leapt up and grabbed the young agent's lapel.

'Ahhhhhhhhh!!!' yelled Jay, freaking out. 'He's alive! *HE'S STILL ALIVE*!!!'

'I said *most* of his bodily fluids,' said Elle, attaching a high-tech drip to the arm.

'It's okay, you're in good hands,' she said to the tourist. Then she turned to Kay and Jay. 'It's like something tried to suck the life-force out of him.'

Jay caught his breath. 'Straight talking. Perp's M.O.?'

'Unknown,' said Kay as he studied the diagnostic photos. 'Despite what the media would have you believe, aliens rarely assault humans.'

Elle showed them another photo, showing a colour-coded glow around the victim's neck. 'Found a puncture wound.'

'Maybe our alien's from Transylvania,' said Jay.

Kay reached into the tourist's shirt pocket and took out the business card.

'Maybe he drives a cab,' he said.

An MiB limo pulled up in front of the Lone Wolf Cab Company. Jay and Kay stepped out to see a row of cabs lined up in front of the garage area and several cabbies milling around.

Forbus sat by himself, looking surly. He looked up, saw the Men in Black and ran towards his cab.

Kay whipped out his standard issue Raygun, aimed at the running cabbie and yelled, *'Stop!!!'*

But Jay ran right across his line of sight. 'Ruined my shot, Slick,' said Kay.

Aware that Jay was gaining on him, Forbus ran right past his cab.

Kay, regaining his cool, walked briskly behind as Jay took a flying leap at Forbus and wrestled him into submission.

But Forbus morphed into his awful Alcidian self, causing Jay to recoil in surprise and revulsion. The alien took advantage of the moment and flipped Jay over his head. But the young agent rose quickly and whipped out his Noisy Cricket gun.

'Freeze!' he yelled, while spinning the alien against the wall and cautiously frisking him. 'Okay, turn real slow.'

Kay arrived on the scene. 'An *Alcidian*?' he said, as a mouth-like suction cup opened on the alien's hand.

'Slick! Heads up!' yelled Kay, rushing over as Forbus made a grab for Jay and knocked the Noisy Cricket out of his hand.

Forbus then turned on Kay and clasped his hand in a suction-cup grip. Kay groaned and passed out.

Jay glanced between his fallen friend and Forbus who was now stumbling towards his cab. Jay rushed to Kay, as the alien gunned the engine and sped away.

Jay checked out the circular puncture wound on Kay's palm. He whipped out his Communicator and held it to his lips.

'Man down!' he said.

Still unconscious, Kay was wheeled into the MiB Emergency Ward.

'Kay, don't raisin up on me, man,' said Jay, walking beside the stretcher as it was pushed into a room where Elle waited.

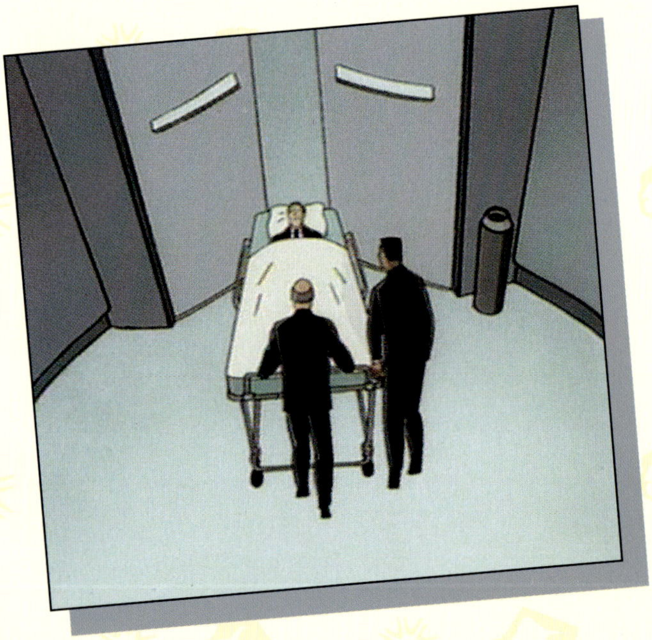

'Do something!' said Jay.

Elle simply gave Kay a shot and he instantly sat up.

'Like that?' said Elle.

'Packed a wallop for an Alcidian handshake,' said Kay.

'Whoa, Kay. Lie back, take it easy,' said Jay, fussing over his partner. 'Er...what's an Alcidian handshake?'

Kay stood and brushed himself off. 'Alcidians are extremely sociable beings,' he said. 'They exchange some of their "essence" by biting each other's hands...kind of a bonding experience, creates an emotional link.'

'Is it dangerous?' asked Jay.

Kay and Elle exchanged knowing looks.

'Not if you're an Alcidian,' said Elle.

'Alcidians don't press flesh with humans,' said Kay. 'Our friend seems to be the exception.'

'Okay,' said Jay. 'So he's some sort of alien sociopath. Why didn't he just shrivel you up like the other guy?'

'I don't have what he's looking for in a victim.'

'Self-defence, then?' said Jay.

'No,' said Kay. 'Too pre-meditated. He's up to something.'

In a deserted alleyway Forbus stood beside his cab. He glanced around, made sure the coast was clear, then opened the bonnet. He bent over the engine and flicked a switch near the steaming radiator. The cab suddenly morphed into a gleaming black sedan, and the numbers on its licence plate scrambled to a different combination.

He was about to close the bonnet when he paused, reached out a hand and pressed it onto the steaming radiator. There was a horrible hissing noise and he grimaced with pain...but he still managed an evil chuckle.

At *exactly* the same moment, Kay grabbed *his* wrist and writhed in agony.

'Kay, what happened?' asked Jay.

Kay shook his hand as the pain subsided. 'Our perp just sent me a message.'

'How? What did he say?'

'Whatever happens to him, happens to me,' said Kay. 'We can't touch him without touching me. A defensive version of that "bonding experience" I was telling you about.'

'Too bad it's not going to work,' said Elle, wheeling some high-tech equipment over to Kay. 'A transfusion will clear the Alcidian essence from your bloodstream.'

'No,' said Kay, waving Elle away. 'Our Alcidian might strike again. And if I can feel his pain, who knows what else I might experience?'

'So you're saying you and he are like the Corsican Brothers?' asked Jay, as the two MiB agents stepped out of the limo outside an old-fashioned diner.

'Except we're *not* brothers,' said Kay. 'Otherwise, you're exactly right...Here's where the Alcidian cabbies hang out. Only place in town that specialises in their cuisine.'

'Guy you're talking about sounds like Forbus...' said an Alcidian cabbie seated in a large booth with two green-eyed companions. '...Nobody wants to shake hands with Forbus.'

'He's anti-social...'

'...Talks to himself...'

'...Eats human food...'

'...Yeeeeuchhh!'

'Know where I can find him?' asked Kay.

'No, I got a photo, though,' said the cabbie, handing Kay a snapshot.

Just then another Alcidian came in. As the others stood up to greet him, suction-cup mouths appeared on their hands and they exchanged High Fives.

'...Good to see you, Newt.'

'...Have a seat...'

'...How's it going?'

As the Alcidians sat down, Kay and Jay studied the photo. It was a group picture of the cabbies in the restaurant, with Forbus at his own table off to the side. He was covering his face in horror and repulsion.

'He totally freaked out,' said the first Alcidian.

'Maybe he was having a bad hair day,' suggested Jay.

The second Alcidian shook his head. 'He broke my camera. Did this to me...'

Jay gasped in horror as the second Alcidian pulled down his collar and revealed a hideous open wound from behind his ear down to his collar bone.

'Not as bad as it looks. Just tore the suit,' said the alien. 'Haven't seen him since.'

The waitress came up to the table and served Jay and Kay with two sandwiches. Then she placed a big bowl of steaming, lumpy gruel in front of the Alcidians.

'The usual,' she said, 'and two tuna melts.'

The Alcidians stared at the sandwiches and muttered among themselves. 'Human food...'

'...I believe they *eat* that stuff...'

Then they dug into the gruel with their bare hands.

'When in Rome...' said Kay, taking a dip into the gruel. 'Not bad. Tastes like a Fredo's pizza.'

At exactly the same moment, Forbus' black sedan was parked outside Fredo's Pizzeria – and Forbus was biting into a pizza as he sat at the window.

'Give me some of that,' said Jay, looking on with fascination as Kay continued to eat the gruesome gruel.

He took a bite and spat it out in disgust. 'That tastes *so not* like a Fredo's.'

Realisation suddenly dawned on Kay. 'You're right!'

At that moment a professional photographer walked past Fredo's, looked up at the bright neon sign and took a picture of it.

Forbus saw this, dropped his pizza and ducked down. His green eyes were seething with rage and hatred as he covered his head.

The MiB's souped-up limo sped along the highway like a flash. Kay, at the wheel, suddenly ducked and covered his head. The car jerked back and forth across the highway as Jay grabbed the steering wheel and yanked on the brakes.

The limo zipped off the road, snapped a STOP sign, screeched to a halt and finally came to rest.

Kay sat back, blinking.

Jay looked mortified. 'Maybe *I* should drive,' he said.

Kay brushed him off. 'I'm okay, I just felt "violated"...and now I have to...hurt someone.'

The professional photographer was getting into his car, when the hate-filled Forbus suddenly leapt right through Fredo's window.

As the petrified photographer gunned the engine and sped away, he looked in the rear-view mirror and saw Forbus chasing him on foot. The photographer put his foot down and pulled away from the alien.

Then Forbus got into the sedan and sped off after the car.

In the safety of his darkroom the photographer developed his photos then hung them up to dry. Each one showed a 1950s neon sign, like the one outside Fredo's Pizzeria.

Suddenly the door creaked open.

'What the...?' he said.

Forbus stood there, transforming into his wild-eyed Alcidian self. He lunged forward and grabbed the photographer by the side of his neck. The man screamed, as the photo of Fredo's Pizzeria was slowly developing in a tray.

The hanging red lamp smashed down into the developer and erupted into flames!

The photo image of Forbus shielding his eyes in the pizzeria, was engulfed by fire.

The limo screeched to a halt outside Fredo's. Jay and Kay looked around but Forbus was nowhere to be seen.

'Maybe he got a take-out,' said Jay.

Just then Kay began convulsing with violent coughs. His eyes watered, he broke into a heavy sweat and grabbed at his throat.

'Kay, what is it?' asked Jay.

'Smoke, burning...'

Jay looked around and shrugged. There was no fire to be seen. Then they glanced at one another in alarm – and rushed outside.

'There!' said Kay, pointing to a plume of smoke rising from a building a few blocks away.

They leapt back into the limo and headed for the fire.

Jay and Kay fought their way through the smoke- and flame-filled studio. They managed to pull the photographer out, but he now resembled a skinny shrivelled toothpick.

Then the ceiling collapsed in a heap of glowing embers. The burning debris blocked the doorway, trapping them all inside.

Jay's eyes were watery. He was coughing and sweating. Yet, amazingly, Kay remained as cool as ever.

'Strange,' he said. 'It's a cool heat... Let me guess – Forbus has left the building.'

Indeed, a cool breeze was blowing up on the roof where Forbus was climbing out of a ventilation shaft.

Kay fired his "icer" and iced the flames – stopping their molecules and freeze-framing them.

Elle and some MiB aides were waiting outside. Jay and Kay handed the poor photographer over to her.

'Get this man on a Quanuvian drip!' she ordered.

Then they spotted Forbus leaping into his sedan and screeching off. Kay and Jay leapt into the limo and sped after him.

'He's at least running scared,' said Jay.

Forbus zig-zagged through traffic, smoothly negotiating turns at high speed and whipping down side streets.

The MiB vehicle kept pace with the Alcidian. Then, at a fork in the road, the sedan made a sudden dash across three lanes of traffic and took off.

Kay was caught off guard by this manoeuvre. He missed the fork, screeched the limo to a halt, backed up and saw the sedan way ahead in the distance.

'Time for overdrive,' he said, reaching down for *the button.*

'I'll get the seat belt,' said Jay.

Kay hit the button and Jay was thrown back in his seat, as the limo transformed into a Supercar and took off in a flash, humming and pulsating with its wheels a couple of feet off the road.

A moment later the limo was alongside the sedan. Kay opened his window, reached out and knocked on Forbus' front passenger window. Forbus rolled the window down.

'You are in violation of Statute five-o-four of the Triton Accord,' said Kay. 'Surrender peaceably.'

Then he turned to Jay and said 'Duck!'

Forbus fired a huge Raygun right at them and both agents ducked just in time.

'You *knew* that was coming,' said Jay, as they lifted their heads again.

'Call it a hunch,' shrugged Kay.

Jay bounced around trying to get his seat belt on, as Kay steered through back roads before skidding to a stop right in front of the oncoming sedan which Forbus had now transformed into a Supercar. Jay looked up and saw it coming straight at them.

'Kayyyyyyyy....'

'Now he's scared,' said Kay.

Forbus gasped in fear, slammed his foot on the brake and spun the steering wheel. Tyres screeched, then the sedan flipped through the air and landed in a spectacular crash.

'Never mind,' said Jay, tossing the unfastened seat belt aside.

Steam hissed from the wrecked sedan/Supercar and it shrank back to its original cab form, as though it were dying.

A moment later Forbus leapt out unharmed, and started running.

Jay took off after him with typical gung-ho bravado. Kay followed, coolly.

Jay caught up with the Alcidian, took a flying leap and tackled him to the ground.

Forbus groaned and held his side, flailing around as Jay tried to pin him down.

'Kay, back up!' called Jay.

But when he turned around again he was alarmed to see his partner down on his knees and groaning in pain.

'Nice punch, Slick...finish him off,' said Kay.

Jay drew his fist back to deliver a powerful blow to Forbus – but then he froze.

Forbus chuckled as Jay glanced back and forth, knowing if he delivered the blow, then Kay would feel the pain.

Forbus took advantage of the moment. He threw Jay onto his back and darted off again, disappearing into the traffic.

'Told you to finish him off,' said Kay. 'Had a feeling he was gonna hurt *you* more than you hurt *me!*'

A fire engine was parked in front of the photographer's studio, and a few firemen were extinguishing the remaining embers.

Kay and Jay hopped out of the limo, beside the MiB Clean-Up van. Elle was inside the van taking strobe pictures of the photographer. She climbed out and closed the door behind her.

Kay looked up at the charred photo studio sign. 'A camera-wielding tourist, a photographer...'

'He's after people who take his picture,' said Jay.

'Bingo!' said Kay.

A TV news van screeched up to the scene. A cameraman leapt out and began filming the building. 'Anybody see what happened here!?' he asked, turning his camera to Jay and Kay. 'How about *you?!*'

Kay immediately turned his head, shielded his eyes – and freaked out!

'Get that thing out of my face!' he yelled, rushing up to the cameraman and knocking his camera to the ground.

Jay and Elle pulled Kay away. He was holding his chest and breathing heavily. 'I feel drained,' he said.

'Like someone's taken your essence?' said Elle.

'Yes,' groaned Kay.

'Forbus is on some weird "eye for an eye" jag, isn't he?' said Jay. 'Doing to others what he *thinks* they're doing to him.'

Elle nodded. 'He's definitely psychotic...and Kay's identifying with him is starting to concern me.'

She opened the van door. 'Kay, you're going back to headquarters for an emergency transfusion.'

Kay motioned to Jay and began to head back to the limo.

'No, I'm too close,' he said. 'I'm the only one who can stop Forbus.'

It was dusk. Kay looked haggard as he drove the limo in another part of town. Elle sat in the back seat.

'I hope you don't mind if I keep you under observation,' she said, watching him closely.

'Suit yourself,' replied Kay.

'So, what happens if you get too far inside Forbus' head?' Jay asked Kay.

'You're both professionals. If I cross that line, you'll know what to do,' Kay replied.

Elle and Jay exchanged apprehensive glances.

In Times Square, Forbus shuffled along looking haggard and intense. As he stepped into the bright lights, he was caught by a video camera and his image appeared on the huge screen overlooking the square.

Forbus looked up at the screen, broke into a sweat and covered his face with his arms.

At the wheel of the limo, Kay covered his eyes too.

'I just wish he'd let me drive,' said Jay, as the vehicle spun to a stop.

'It's happening again,' said Kay.

The wild-eyed Forbus was panting and looking around frantically. He spotted a video cameraman filming the crowd from the top of a building.

Knocking people out the way, Forbus walked across the square and began climbing the side of the building.

A couple of cops were sipping coffee as they leaned against their car. They looked up, saw Forbus, dropped their coffee and ran through the crowd towards him.

'Hey,' said the cameraman up on the roof as Forbus hoisted himself up. 'Who are..?'

Forbus lunged at him, and hurled the video camera to the ground. Then he morphed into his Alcidian self...but immediately de-morphed back to human form as the two cops arrived on the scene.

'Hold it...don't move!' they yelled.

As Forbus turned, the cameraman ran away to safety.

More cops arrived, their pistols trained on Forbus.

'Go on, *shoot*,' said Forbus. 'The innocent will perish.'

The cops exchanged shaky, uncertain glances.

In the limo, Kay's head was reeling. He was panting and sweating.

'He's close...I can feel it!' he said, slamming on the brakes.

Jay looked up and saw the giant screen in Times Square. On it was Forbus – throwing policemen to and fro, like ragdolls.

Forbus ran off as even more police poured onto the rooftop.

'Halt!' yelled the police captain.

But the Alcidian kept running.

Jay and Elle arrived on the roof just as the police were raising their rifles.

'If they shoot Forbus...' said Elle.

'...they shoot Kay!' said Jay, waving his arms and making a mad dash in front of the policemen. 'Stop! Don't fire!'

'Get out of there,' yelled the captain. 'This is a restricted...'

The captain recognised Jay. 'Detective Edwards?' he said, in some surprise.

'I've, uuh...been working deep cover,' said Jay, awkwardly. 'Deep, deep, deep cover. This is my collar and I need him alive.'

The captain hesitated, then raised his megaphone and ordered his men to hold fire.

In his human form, Forbus ran across the rooftops and leapt from building to building – until he came face to face with Kay.

'Forbus,' said Kay, pulling out his carboniser, '...say "cheese".'

Forbus walked slowly towards Kay – and morphed into his hideous alien form.

'Shooting me,' he chuckled evilly, 'would be shooting yourself.'

He stepped closer and transmitted his thoughts into Kay's brain. *'We're bonded, you and I...'*

Kay reeled and lowered his gun, as Forbus' thoughts echoed in his head. *'...I'm within you. Your head, your soul. Can you feel me? You know those who steal our essence must perish. You know you must let me escape.'*

As Forbus took another step forward, Kay raised the carboniser again.

'No!' he shouted.

Jay and Elle heard the carboniser's blast.

They looked up and saw two figures on a rooftop, silhouetted against the city lights. Then they gasped as the figures dropped like dead-weights.

Up on the roof they discovered Kay, then they turned to see Forbus hobble onto the access stairwell.

'The good news is, *he's* not dead either,' said Elle.

She looked Kay over. There were no blast wounds. She opened her medical kit, revealing the diagnostic camera and vials of serum as she prepared an injection.

Jay leapt to his feet, his Noisy Cricket at the ready, and chased after Forbus. He reached the bottom of the stairway and looked around. The interior of the building was dark. There were lots of dimly lit offices, stairways, elevators and corridors. Jay skulked through the shadows, stopped at the doorway of an office and stepped inside.

Forbus was crouched in a dark corner. Jay slowly approached him, holding his arms out to show that he meant no harm.

'Forbus...stay cool. I just want to get you to a doctor,' he said.

'Eyes are...windows of the soul,' mumbled Forbus. 'Demonic devices...steal my essence...'

Out on the roof, Kay was delirious too.

'Demonic devices...steal my essence...'

Elle injected him with the serum – and his eyes blinked open.

'Don't move, Kay,' she said, holding the diagnostic camera. 'I want to do a diagnostic to make sure there's no internal injuries.'

As she pointed the camera at him, Kay knocked her aside. Then he stood over her, menacingly.

'You tried to...steal from me,' he said.

'C'mon...' said Jay, attemping to haul Forbus to his feet.

The alien's green eyes suddenly blinked open. He grabbed Jay, lifted him over his head and flung him across the corridor.

Jay stumbled to his feet, as Forbus attacked him again, grabbing him and smashing him against the wall, then flinging him down a staircase.

Jay stumbled to his feet again, in time to see Forbus chuckling to himself as he casually left the room.

Elle was backing away from Kay as he loomed over her.

'Look into your soul, Kay. It's a *human* soul... If you don't look into your soul right now,' said Elle, 'I may have to hurt you.'

Then her eyes widened in alarm as Kay aimed his carboniser at her. She lashed out, kicked his feet from under him, then made a dive for the stairwell access.

But Forbus blocked her path. Elle backed away from him, right into Kay, who had the carboniser at her back.

'Do what I would do,' said Forbus. 'Pull the trigger.'

'Kay, *don't*...' it was Jay, wounded and hanging onto the access door for support. He was pointing the Noisy Cricket at Kay. 'I'll shoot him...shoot *you*.'

Kay simply looked at Forbus and smiled a broad smile.

Jay looked at Forbus. 'Make him let her go!'

'You won't shoot,' said Forbus. 'You know it. I know it...' He nodded at Kay, '...he knows it.'

'Kay's already gone, man,' said Jay, trying to figure whether Forbus meant it or not. 'If he was still here, he'd do the *same thing!!!*'

'Would he...?'

Jay hesitated. He was wavering when Elle spoke up. 'Do it, Jay...' She glanced down at her feet, *'...shoot!'*

With that she kicked her foot through the strap of the diagnostic camera and flung it into the air.

Jay dropped the Noisy Cricket and caught the camera. He aimed it straight at Forbus' face and released the shutter. The flash gun flashed and both Forbus and Kay screamed, covering their faces and falling to their knees.

Elle took the opportunity to whip out a hypo from her bag and give them both knock-out shots.

As they slipped into unconsciousness, Jay quipped, 'Joke's on them...lens cap's still on.'

Kay and Forbus lay beside one another in the MiB medical ward. They were connected by a series of tubes and high-tech machines operated by Elle as Jay stood by and watched.

The tourist and the photographer were laying on nearby tables, restored back to health by MiB attendants, who slipped on shades and flashed a Neuralyser in their eyes.

'This transfusion will return all essences to their original owners,' said Elle.

'What about Forbus?' said Jay.

'MiB mental ward,' she said. 'We can help him.'

A few days later, Jay and Kay watched the Alcidian cab drivers eating their tubs of gruel in the old-fashioned diner.

'Partake?' offered one of the Alcidians.

Kay and Jay gestured 'no thanks' as a waitress set plates of sandwiches in front of them.

'Thanks, we'll stick with the tuna melts,' said Kay.

'I'm reading your mind, partner,' agreed Jay.

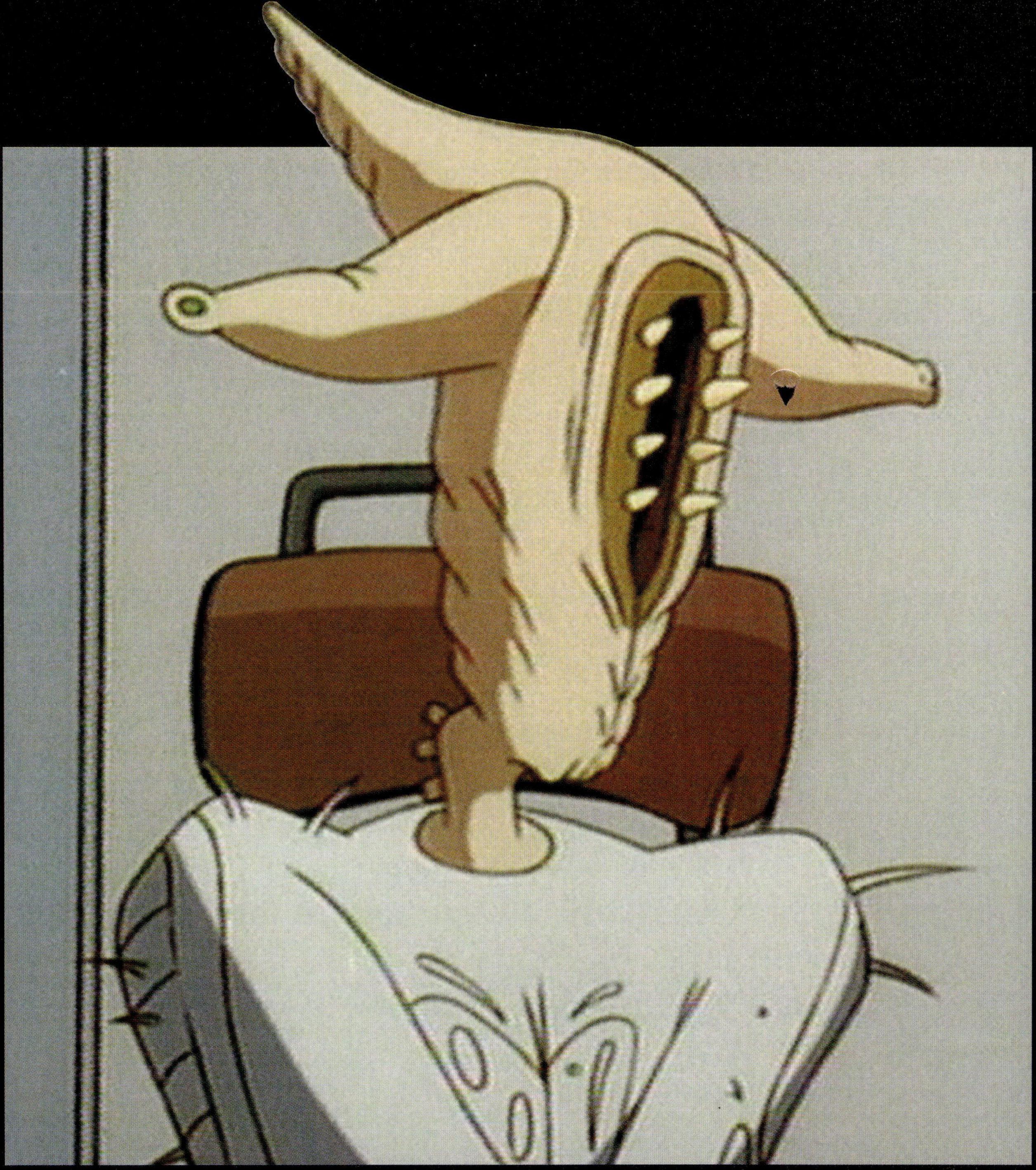

At that very moment in the MiB mental ward, Forbus was undergoing a Rorschach test. The blob on the card resembled a dog.

'I see a tuna melt,' he said.

'Interesting,' said the MiB psychologist.

Then she showed him another Rorschach card. This one looked a bit like a shapely babe.

'And here?'

'Tuna melt,' said Forbus. 'Definitely a tuna melt.'

THE MiB DRESS CODE

- Black suit, must be dry-cleaned after each assignment
- White shirt
- Black tie
- Black socks
- Black shoes (style at agent's discretion)
- Black sunglasses
- Boxer shorts – always clean (in case agent is involved in an accident)
- Hair must be kept neat and inconspicuous
- Agents must shave daily (beard or moustache to be approved by supervisor)

MiB WEAPONS

MiB agents are always armed and ready for battle while on duty...

CARBONISER

Discharges Carbon X-11, an alien gas so powerful it would vaporise human flesh in 12 seconds. Has a fogging radius of 100 feet.

NOISY CRICKET

Tiny handgun, but very, very powerful.

SERIES 4 DE-ATOMISER

Triple-barrelled shot-gun with five settings. Can be used as a squirt gun, a sling shot, a BB gun, a bazooka or an atomic machine gun. Requires a six-week training course.

THE NEURALYSER

An indispensable tool for the MiB. The Neuralyser emits laser light that can penetrate the human skull and block memory impulses to the brain. If a human accidentally witnesses alien activity, the Neuralyser may be used to erase that memory.

MiB TRANSPORTATION

The Men in Black travel in a fleet of specially equipped limousines. These incredible vehicles, powered by certified rocket fuel, are housed in the agency's Autoport on sub-level five. They have a number of unusual functions...

- Speeds in excess of 400 mph are possible
- Laughing Gas can be emitted from the exhaust pipe to disable aliens within a 30-foot radius
- Floatable tyres are fitted – will activate when the car is in more than two feet of water
- Bullet-proof windscreen, with automatic squeegees to clean away bugs
- Three beam positions on headlights: low, high and super-high

HOW THE MiB CAUGHT A TRETSVEN IN THE TUNNEL OF LOVE...

It was night time at the carnival. Everyone was having a real good time, amid the bright lights.

Kay and Jay were floating in a little boat through the Tunnel of Love. They were searching for an alien – a Tretsven.

Jay looked anxious, nervous. 'You sure it's not the Bearded Lady? There's definitely something alien about her.'

Kay shook his head. 'She's a regular taxpayer,' he said.

'I feel kinda weird about this,' admitted Jay.

'All part of the job, Slick.'

The little boat bobbed into the Tunnel which was lit every few feet by cheesy red lights. Tinny romantic music wafted through the air.

Once inside, Kay and Jay hopped off the boat and moved into the shadows.

'What makes you so sure it's coming through here?' whispered Jay.

'Dark...secluded...' said Kay. 'This is where I'd go.'

'Didn't know you were such a romantic.'

A boat carrying a clean-cut young couple approached. They seemed to be very much in love.

The girl closed her eyes waiting for the kiss. But instead of going for the big smooch, the young man morphed into a hideous, bestial alien with razor sharp fangs.

The girl opened her eyes and screamed!

Then the alien fell as Kay splatted him with a Raygun.

'That was no cupid's arrow,' observed Jay.

'Had no choice,' said Kay. '*Tretsvens* don't break hearts...they *eat* them.'

He hopped into the boat to comfort the girl who looked up at him.

'To think I loved him,' she said.

Kay pulled on his shades and took out a Neuralyser.

'Ma'am...you'll get over Romeo quicker than you think.'

And the Neuralyser flashed.

THE FAREWELL SYNDROME

Based on the episode "The Farewell Syndrome" written by Tom Pugsley & Greg Klein
Based on the Malibu Comic by Lowell Cunningham

Warren, a young night-watchman, sat outside his booth on an Industrial Park in Jersey. It was a hot summer's night and he was watching a tiny portable TV on which a cheesy 'alien' was about to jump on an 'agent'.

'Dude, behind you...' Warren yelled at the screen.

Just then the lights began to flicker and the TV screen went fuzzy. As Warren tried adjusting the set, the lights went out completely.

Then some sort of projectile zoomed overhead and made a soft, controlled landing beyond the warehouses.

After a moment's hesitation, Warren reached for his flashlight, clicked it on and ventured into the darkness at the side of the building.

On the other side of the Industrial Park lay a small, car-sized spacecraft, smouldering slightly in the dirt. It began to morph. Its hardware became organic, pink and spongy. It had tentacles and a hideous face and its breath came heavily as it slinked and slithered away.

Warren thought he heard something. 'Uhhh....who goes there?' he said nervously, as his torch beam scanned the empty darkness. But he saw nothing.

Then all the lights clicked on again and he returned to the booth.

Warren sat down in front of the TV and watched with enthusiasm for a moment. Then he turned and found himself looking at a second, *identical* chair sitting beside him.

'Hey, that wasn't there...'

The armrests of the chair he was sitting on suddenly came to life and pinned his arms down. Then the chair's legs began to wrap themselves around his feet, and the chair back elongated itself vertically, wrapped itself around his head and held him like a vice.

Warren screamed as sharp Venus Fly Trap-like teeth formed from within the texture of the chair and prepared to bite his head. *This chair was alive!*

Then, from the near distance, a car's headlights pierced the darkness and hit the chair. It instantly separated itself from Warren and scuttled off into the darkness.

Kay and Jay were riding in the limo as it crossed the Industrial Park.

'Co-ordinates verified,' said Kay. 'Bogey landed here.'

'Gotta be a crash landing,' said Jay.

'Logic?'

'Nobody *wants* to go to Jersey.'

'Maybe *he* knows someone.'

Up ahead, in the headlights' beams, they saw Warren crawling into view and looking like he'd just seen a ghost.

Later, back at MiB headquarters, Kay and Jay headed for Zed's office.

'Can't believe we spent two hours looking for a *chair*,' said Jay.

'Yet not a chair,' said Kay. 'An amazing *simulation*.'

Zed was sitting at his desk.

'Slick and I took stock of the Jersey landing,' said Kay. 'We're dealing with an...'

'...Inanimate,' interrupted a female voice.

Kay and Jay turned to see Agent Aileen standing beside them. She was gorgeous with a perfect body clad in a designer black suit.

'...an EkoVees, to be exact,' she continued. 'Because of the nature of sub-atomic matter in its galaxy, it can manipulate its molecules to mimic any inanimate object it touches.'

Jay was awe-struck by the new babe

on the block. 'Haven't seen her before,' he muttered.

Kay remained poker-faced. 'She's not local,' he said.

'Agent Aileen will be working with us on this case,' said Zed.

Jay swaggered in and shook her hand. 'I'm Jay. Nice to see a fresh human face after dealing with butt-ugly aliens all day.'

'Really,' replied Aileen, slipping a blue-skinned tendril into his coat. 'Some of my best friends are aliens.'

'Hey!' said Jay, as Aileen's 'arm' pulled the Noisy Cricket from his jacket.

'Of course, talk like this can be a bit *disarming*,' said Aileen. 'Shall we stick to business, *Agent* Jay?'

'Yes, ma'am,' said Jay, gaping in awe.

Aileen returned the Noisy Cricket and the tendril slithered up her sleeve, then re-emerged as a human hand.

Kay turned to Jay. 'Told you she wasn't local.'

Kay remained poker-faced as his eyes met Aileen's.

'Good to see you again, Kay,' she said.

'You know him?' asked Jay.

'Intimately,' replied Aileen.

Jay was stunned and confused.

'She's talking about the *perp*,' said Kay.

'Of course,' said Aileen. 'Typical scum of the universe. Murder, intergalactic extortion. Recently busted free of Zartacla maximum security prison.'

Jay chuckled. 'Lemme guess – it *mimicked* a cake with a file inside and sawed its way out?'

All three glared at him.

'Don't let its looks fool you,' said Aileen. 'The EkoVees is one of the most ruthless beings I've encountered...I would know. It took my partner.'

'Er...so why *Earth*?' said Jay, quickly changing the subject. 'Why *New York*?'

'Unknown,' said Aileen. 'But not because it wants to see the Statue of Liberty.'

'Kay and I will show it some sights,' said Jay confidently.

Zed looked at Jay. 'Son, due to Aileen's familiarity with the Inanimate, I'm temporarily partnering her with Kay.'

'What!??!' said Jay.

'Like old times,' said Aileen.

'Wait a minute,' said Jay. 'What about me?'

'You'll be partnered with U,' said Zed.

'Going solo!? I get lonesome,' complained Jay.

'Not *you*,' said Zed. 'U – *Agent U*.'

Agent U came in. He was the agency's most by-the-book operator. 'Sir!' he said.

Zed turned to Jay with a little wry grin. 'You and U will be working on a...special assignment.'

'Great idea, as usual, Sir,' said U. 'That's why *you're* Mr MiB!'

Jay eyed U with disbelief. The guy scared him.

Jay's 'special assignment' was to assist Agent U, in teaching a class of alien school kids. They were of all shapes and sizes, and they were all *bored*.

Jay was holding up an easel with 'Welcome to Earth' written on it. Agent U was dressed in an Auxy the Centipede outfit.

'Hi, Kids,' said U. 'I'm Auxy, the Auxionbus centipede.'

Music played, and U rocked with the beat.

'Now, to help you remember how to act human here on planet Earth, Auxy and Agent Jay are going to sing you a little song...'

Jay just looked sick.

Kay was driving the limo with Aileen beside him.

'Sorry to hear about Pheelobar,' he said.

'He was a good cop,' said Aileen. 'I'll be thinking about him when I bring down the Inanimate.'

'Something that can be *anything*, will stop at *nothing*,' said Kay.

'Reminds me of that crazed Villivavian, remember?' she said.

'Who could forget wrestling a four-thousand pound Pus worm?'

'Who could forget hitting the showers afterwards?'

Kay nodded at the memory. 'Took hours to wash away the ick.'

'I know,' said Aileen. 'I was there.'

There was a moment of awkward silence between them. Then Aileen spoke again. 'Time to face facts. With Pheelobar gone, there's a void that needs to be filled.'

'Anyone in mind?' asked Kay.

Jay was watching Kay and Aileen through high-tech binoculars from Agent U's car. 'Definitely something different 'bout him... Got it! Tie's tied with a full-on Waverly knot. He never ties it that way around me.'

'Agent Jay,' said an astonished U. 'Unauthorised departure from an assignment is a violation. Haven't you read the manual?'

'Waiting for the movie, *Upton*.'

'*Code names are classified!!*' spluttered U. *'How did you know??'*

'Your letter's "U", you don't look like an Ursula...now keep your eyes peeled for any suspicious looking sofa beds or loungers...'

'"Eyes"?' said Frank. 'No...I'm a Pug, see.'

Kay and Aileen raised their eyebrows.

'Ladies first,' said Kay.

Aileen grabbed Frank and shook him, firmly. 'Be a good doggy... speak.'

'Can't...choking me,' said Frank as his eyes bulged.

'My hands are nowhere near your...' she said. Then she noticed that the pug was wearing two identical collars – and one of them was constricting.

She put Frank back on the counter and whipped out her Raygun. Kay did the same, as the Pug continued to make choking sounds.

'Let go *now*!!' said Aileen.

'Hurt the dog, go down screaming!' said Kay.

The constricting collar continued to choke the Pug.

Then, so sudden that Aileen and Kay were taken by surprise, the Inanimate sprung free of Frank's neck and morphed in 'mid-air' into a spongy, tentacled body with a grotesque face – if you could call it a *face!*

The creature spluttered in incomprehensible alienese.

The limo screeched up to a news-stand. Frank the Pug was at the counter. His human partner stood off to the side, typically catatonic.

'Frank, been a while,' said Aileen.

'Aileen,' said the Pug, looking very, very nervous. '...Uhh nice to see you.'

Kay and Aileen exchanged deadpan glances. Frank was *never* that nice.

'We're looking for an Inanimate,' said Aileen.

Frank gestured to his partner. 'Talk to him, he hasn't moved in days.'

Every now and then Frank's eyes darted behind him, as if he were trying to alert them to something. 'Gee...nothing to tell,' he said. 'Nope, not a thing.'

'Something wrong with your eyes?' asked Aileen, leaning forward.

In Agent U's car, Jay tore the clip-on binoculars from his glasses.

'Whoa!' he said. 'Let's move!'

Jay and U leapt out ready to spring into action.

Frank the Pug, now wearing just one collar, was trying to catch his breath.

'What did it want?!!' asked Aileen.

'Dunno,' said Frank. 'It was asking questions...'bout MiB.'

The two agents exchanged glances, then ran off in pursuit of the Inanimate as it skittered across the traffic-lined street. Jay and U followed on behind.

The Inanimate scaled the side of a bus and went right over it in a decidedly *inhuman* way. It landed on the other side without missing a beat. Then it skittered towards a cyclist.

'Look out!' yelled Aileen.

But instead of colliding with the cyclist, the alien morphed into *another* bicycle! Jay and U could hardly believe their eyes as the riderless bike rode into a department store.

As shoppers screamed, Kay and Aileen came in after the bike. They put on their shades as Kay announced: 'Attention shoppers, gather round for a flashing "Blue Light Special".'

Jay and U came in, putting on their shades too.

'We have a sewer leak,' announced Kay. 'Please exit the store single file...'

And the Neuralyser flashed, as terrified shoppers held their noses and ran to the exits.

'Little far from base, Slick,' said Kay to Jay.

'Missed you,' said Jay. 'New tie?'

U stepped forward. 'This was entirely Agent Jay's idea, sir. I tried to communicate that this was against regulations...'

'Unpucker, son,' interrupted Kay. 'Haven't got the time. I want a full sweep...north, south, east, west.'

Moments later Jay was skulking around the menswear department, with his Noisy Cricket at the ready. He passed a row of mannequins all wearing tuxedo-like black suits. He paused by one of the dummies. 'Difference between you and me? he said. 'I make this *look good...*'

Then he spotted a man in a smart hunting outfit walking briskly through the department.

'Hey, *you* heard the man,' snapped

Jay took a few more steps forward, then stopped near a camping display – the mannequin in the display was dressed exactly the same as the man – who was now walking towards him.

'Yo, dummy,' said Jay, leaping at the moving mannequin.

It fell to the ground and its plastic limbs broke off. A leg went one way, the arms another. The head shot straight forward. Jay continued to fight, snapping off the other leg – then he realised that the mannequin was not fighting back.

From ten feet away the mannequin's head stuck its tongue out at Jay then blew a loud raspberry.

It scuttled away on spongy feet and ran to the elevator in the lobby, where it skittered up the wall, tore a ventilation grille right off and climbed inside.

Jay whipped out the Noisy Cricket. 'Yeah. I'll ventilate *you*,' he said, as he hoisted himself up to look inside the ventilator shaft.

The mannequin's head was disappearing around a corner.

Jay climbed into the shaft and began crawling briskly after the Inanimate. But when he reached the corner, the head was nowhere to be seen.

Then there was a loud metallic sound and the shaft began to close in on him. The sudden squeeze forced his hand above his head as he struggled within the tightening steel.

Then an idea came to him – his fingers squeezed the trigger of the Noisy Cricket. The gun went off. Its sound became a deafening echo, and the recoil zipped Jay clean out of the constricting metal and shot him through the shaft like a kid on a thrill ride.

In the lobby, Aileen had to duck as Jay came flying out of the vent shaft.

His momentum caused his shades to fall out of his pocket and slide across the floor.

Then the walls shook, and one of the huge air conditioning units came to life, ripped itself away from the ceiling and pulled its aluminium ducting down to form two spider-like legs.

The monstrous metallic 'spider' swung a 'leg' at Aileen. She tried to leap aside but was struck on the shoulder. Her jacket was ripped, exposing blue translucent skin covering alien muscle and veins.

The 'spider' ripped away a metal panel to expose the whirling fan blades inside. It skulked forward, swiping the blades at Aileen. At the last moment, she turned and kicked out at it, denting the blades – but they ripped through the calf portion of her suit, revealing more blue skin.

Kay came in ready to help Aileen.

'Ready cowboy?' she said.

'Lock, stock and barrel,' said Kay.

They both took out their weapons and released a burst of cannon fire. The beams and blasts ricocheted off the Inanimate. Jay ran in dazed but ready to join the fight.

Badly damaged, the 'spider' slinked around a corner, and Kay and Aileen stopped firing amid clouds of dust and smoke.

Agent U came in and ran to Kay. 'Excellent shooting, Sir. You nicked him...'

Kay just glared at him.

'...a lot' added U.

'He can only sustain harm in his true form,' said Aileen, as they all turned the corner and entered a service corridor.

Jay picked up his shades and slipped them into his jacket. He glared at Aileen. 'How do you lose a 'ten-ton' air conditioning system, that's what I want to know?'

Kay, Jay and Aileen made their way into MiB headquarters.

Let's get you patched up,' said Kay to Aileen.

Agent U confronted Jay. 'I want you to know, I plan on filing a formal complaint regarding your behaviour. You are a disgrace to that suit.'

'Least I'm not a boot-licker,' said Jay, casually removing his shades and putting them away. As he continued down the hall, he didn't notice the shades leap out of his pocket and scuttle away!

In the Interrogation Room Aileen sat on the table, tending to her injured leg. She peeled down her human skin to reveal her real alien skin, glowing a translucent blue.

Kay came in, carrying a cup of steaming coffee in one hand and a jumpsuit on a hanger in the other.

'Sorry, I should have knocked,' he said.

'Always the gentleman,' replied Aileen.

He handed her the cup of coffee. 'Black with two sugars.'

Thanks,' said Aileen. But she didn't drink from the cup. Instead, she poured the hot contents into her leg wound to soothe it!

In the Observation Foyer just outside the Interrogation Room, Jay was watching Kay and Aileen through a one-way-mirror, when Elle came in.

'I tried analysing the pattern of the Inanimate's appearances,' she said, 'but they seem totally random.'

'How are you at reading lips?' said Jay.

Elle looked through the mirror.

Kay spotted an old scar on Aileen's leg. 'Mmm,' he said. 'That's a beaut...'

'Gneescod confrontation,' said Aileen. 'Bit right through a titanium flak suit.'

Kay rolled up his trouser leg to reveal a patch of scarred skin. 'Blevvenite gave me an acid wash,' he said. 'Ruined a good pair of shoes too.'

Aileen smiled. 'I'll see your Blevvenite and raise you a Hotmoth.'

She stripped the 'skin' off her arm to reveal several holes.

Kay was impressed.

'Ow, those sting,' he said, rolling up his sleeve to reveal similar holes in his own skin.

Aileen motioned to the area over her heart. 'This one hurts the most,' she said.

'A heart-eating Tretsven?' said Kay.

'A heart-breaking human,' said Aileen, as the two agents leaned towards one another.

'They're cute together,' said Elle.

Jay gave a petulant frown. 'Don't know what he sees in her.'

'Gee,' said Elle. 'She's only brilliant, a good cop, attractive...'

'Don't be too sure 'bout the last part,' said Jay. 'She's got tentacles. I've seen 'em!'

Kay backed away slightly and lifted the hanger – from which hung a new designer suit and a synthetic human skin!

'Do you want to put this on?' he asked.

Aileen kicked off the rest of her battle-worn human cover. 'In a minute, handsome,' she said.

Her long fingers elongated and entwined to form a tendril which she slinked around Kay's head and pulled him towards her.

'Can't say she's unattractive,' said Elle, watching through the mirror. Then she turned to Jay. 'Know what I think? You're jealous.'

'She lost a partner back on her planet,' he sighed. 'Maybe I don't want to lose mine.'

In the Computer Room, two identical computers sat side by side.

Lots of text and 3-D schematics flashed across one of the screens at dizzying speed, then froze on the plan of a large missile.

Agent U came in and sat in front of the 'live' screen. He began typing, but nothing registered on the screen. Then his fingers sank into the keyboard, as if it were wet cement.

'What the!?!' said U, as the keyboard hardened, trapping his fingers securely.

The screen flashed a message at him. It read: 'GOOD NIGHT'. Then the monitor raised itself up, head-butted him and knocked him out.

As alarms sounded in the Control Centre, the Twins gabbled in unintelligible Alien Speak.

Kay translated. 'There's been a security breach in the mainframe. Someone just downloaded classified files.'

'Or some*thing*,' said Aileen.

They rushed down the hallway and headed for the Computer Room. They found Agent U slumped on the floor. Aileen checked his pulse. 'He's alright, just unconscious.'

Kay logged onto the computer and called up the last file accessed. The plan of the huge missile appeared on the screen.

Kay continued to play the keyboard.

'The Keenanni 6000: an Intergalactic Super Missile the MiB intercepted back in the 'seventies and kept under lock and key. Enough power to annihilate an entire planet.'

'Like mine...' said Aileen.

'He's gonna steal a missile?' said Jay.

'Or *mimic* it,' said Aileen. 'Destruction with a personal touch.'

At the MiB Autoport a guard was questioning Auxy the Centipede. 'C'mon U, you know the drill. I need a voiceprint ID before I can let you through.'

The guard took off the Auxy's head – but there was nothing there. Then the Inanimate's appendages came out of the neck...

‘A guard at the exit was just downed by Auxy the Centipede!’ said Elle.

‘The Inanimate!’ exclaimed Aileen.

Kay stopped Aileen from running off. ‘Needle in a haystack,’ he said. ‘Better bet’s if we beat him there...defuse the missile.’

‘Let him mimic a dud!’ said Aileen.

Kay nodded. ‘Just have to finish printing the schematics...we’ll need the disable code.’

As Kay continued to type at the keyboard, Aileen turned to Jay. ‘Maybe you should pull up the limo. Every second counts.’

‘He’s the only one who drives,’ said Jay.

Unseen by Kay, Aileen’s hand became a blue tendril, slinked into his pocket and whisked the limo keys out. She dangled the keys in front of Jay. He grinned and took them from her.

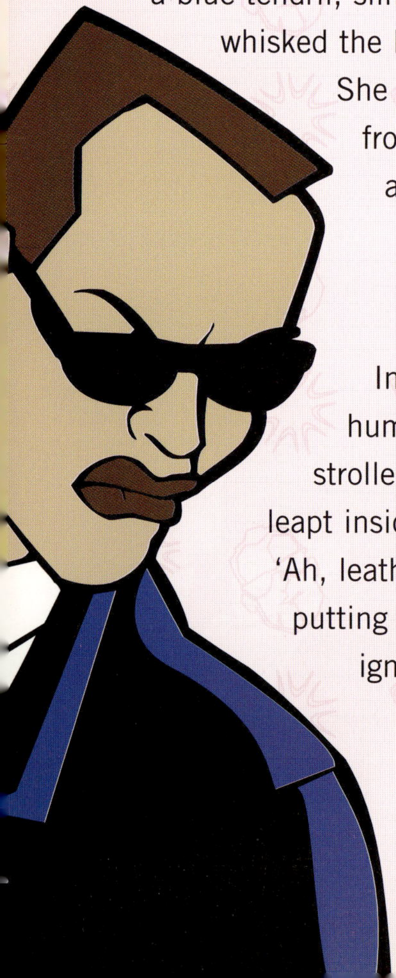

In the Autoport, Jay hummed happily as he strolled up to the limo and leapt inside it.

‘Ah, leather interior...’ he said, putting the key into the ignition.

But the engine started up all by itself... The doors locked all around him... The seat belt threw itself over him and clinched him down tight... The gear stick dropped into drive...and the accelerator pressed itself to the floor.

‘Wha...??!! Hey!!’ yelled Jay.

...and the Inanimate’s ‘face’ pushed out through the dashboard.

To Jay's amazement the figures on the speedometer read *backwards*, so did the frequency numbers on the radio.

Thinking fast, he spied the cigar lighter and shoved it in with his knee. Moments later it popped out with a click, its tip glowing red with heat. He leaned forward, pulled it out with his teeth and pressed it hard onto the dashboard. This caused the Inanimate to emit a loud and angry alien roar and loosen its grip on Jay.

He leapt free of the vehicle and rolled to a stop right in front of an oncoming car which screeched to a halt just a hairbreadth from his skull.

Kay leapt out of the car. 'Difference between that limo and this one?' he said. 'Mine stops on a dime.'

'He's a rookie. He's too *young* to drive!' yelled Kay, as he and Aileen ran into the Autoport.

The vehicle scraped a wall as it sped out of the garage, and it almost ran down some alien attendants.

Kay and Aileen looked around to see the real limo parked beside them.

Jay was scared stiff as the Inanimate/limo barrelled along. He hit the brake pedal, but it disappeared into the floor.

The car screeched around a corner and into a narrow alleyway.

He screamed as he saw a WRONG WAY – DO NOT ENTER sign, and a huge truck heading straight for him.

Then, at the last possible second, the Inanimate/limo threw itself up on two wheels and passed safely between the truck and the building.

Minutes later the *real* limo was in Muscle Car mode and roaring along at top speed in pursuit of the alien copy.

'You do realise that ride was meant for me, don't you, Jay?' asked Aileen.

Jay was sunk low in the back seat like a sulking child. ''Course,' he said.

Kay turned to Aileen. 'Slick's just sulking because you get to ride shotgun.'

At the vault-like door of the Super Missile Silo, two MiB guards were on full alert.

One of them glanced up. 'Hey,' he said. 'What's ceiling tile doing on the wall?'

Suddenly the tiles sprang into life and engulfed the guards.

The limo pulled to a stop beside a run-down ice cream stall.

'So,' said Jay, 'this is where the MiB keeps the most powerful weapon in the galaxy...'

Kay spotted something on the ground. 'Limo tracks. Inanimate's here,' he said.

The tracks of the Inanimate/limo stopped abruptly and changed to tentacle-like footprints leading right up to the back door of the ice cream stand.

Jay climbed down the last few rungs of a ladder to join Kay and Aileen in a circular corridor that surrounded the silo.

'We better split up,' said Kay.

'Have fun playing kissy-face,' said Jay. 'I'll yell if I get ambushed by a drinking fountain.'

'I'll go with Jay,' said Aileen. 'He has a knack for attracting the Inanimate.'

Jay looked surprised as she took him by the elbow.

Jay and Aileen advanced through the corridor, one covering while the other moved to the next position.

'Bet you're anxious to wrap this up and head home?' said Jay.

'If I have a planet to *go home to* when this is over,' replied Aileen.

'Long trip like that must get lonely.'

'No, we'll be in suspended animation,' said Aileen.

'*We?*' said Jay.

'Didn't Kay tell you?'

Kay found the two guards unconscious by the silo door. Then he went inside and saw the impressive ten-storey tall Keenanni 6000 Super Missile.

He scanned the room. The only other equipment in the silo was an oversized computer mainframe with a digital counter above it.

As he moved, he did not see a second steel door as it morphed into the Inanimate.

Kay sensed the movement, but he turned too late. The Inanimate was upon him, wrapping itself around him. His weapon fired into the floor before the alien engulfed him completely.

Jay and Aileen heard the shot and ran towards the sound. They reached the silo in time to see *two* identical Super Missiles.

'Uh, oh,' said Jay.

The digital readout above the mainframe was at 57 seconds – and counting down!

'Which one's which?' said Jay.

Aileen spotted Kay's gun on the floor and called, 'Kay!'

His muffled voice came from inside the Inanimate/Missile. 'In here...disable this thing, pronto...or I'm going on an extended vacation,' he said.

He managed to reach into his pocket and pull out the schematics printout he had taken from MiB headquarters.

Jay and Aileen listened, with their ears pressed against the Inanimate/Missile.

One of the aerodynamic fins came alive and swept Jay and Aileen off their feet – and a large section of the fuselage was about to stomp them like bugs. They rolled away just in time and scrambled to safety.

The countdown clock was at 45 seconds.

Jay pulled out his Noisy Cricket, but Aileen grabbed his hand.

'Too risky,' she said. 'Could blow.'

'Listen up,' said Kay from inside the missile. 'The Keenaani's manual override control panel's about fifty feet up.'

As Jay and Aileen quickly scaled the missile's launch tower, the Inanimate tried to stop them by throwing up all sorts of obstacles that almost threw them off the tower.

But they reached the override panel and Aileen ripped it open with her bare hands. Then the Inanimate grabbed her ankles and pulled her down.

'Keep going,' Aileen yelled at Jay, as a steel rod came to life and whirled like an out-of-control drill bit. It whacked her in the side, but somehow she managed to cling on.

The countdown clock was ticking away...17...16...15... as Jay pulled himself up to the open control panel.

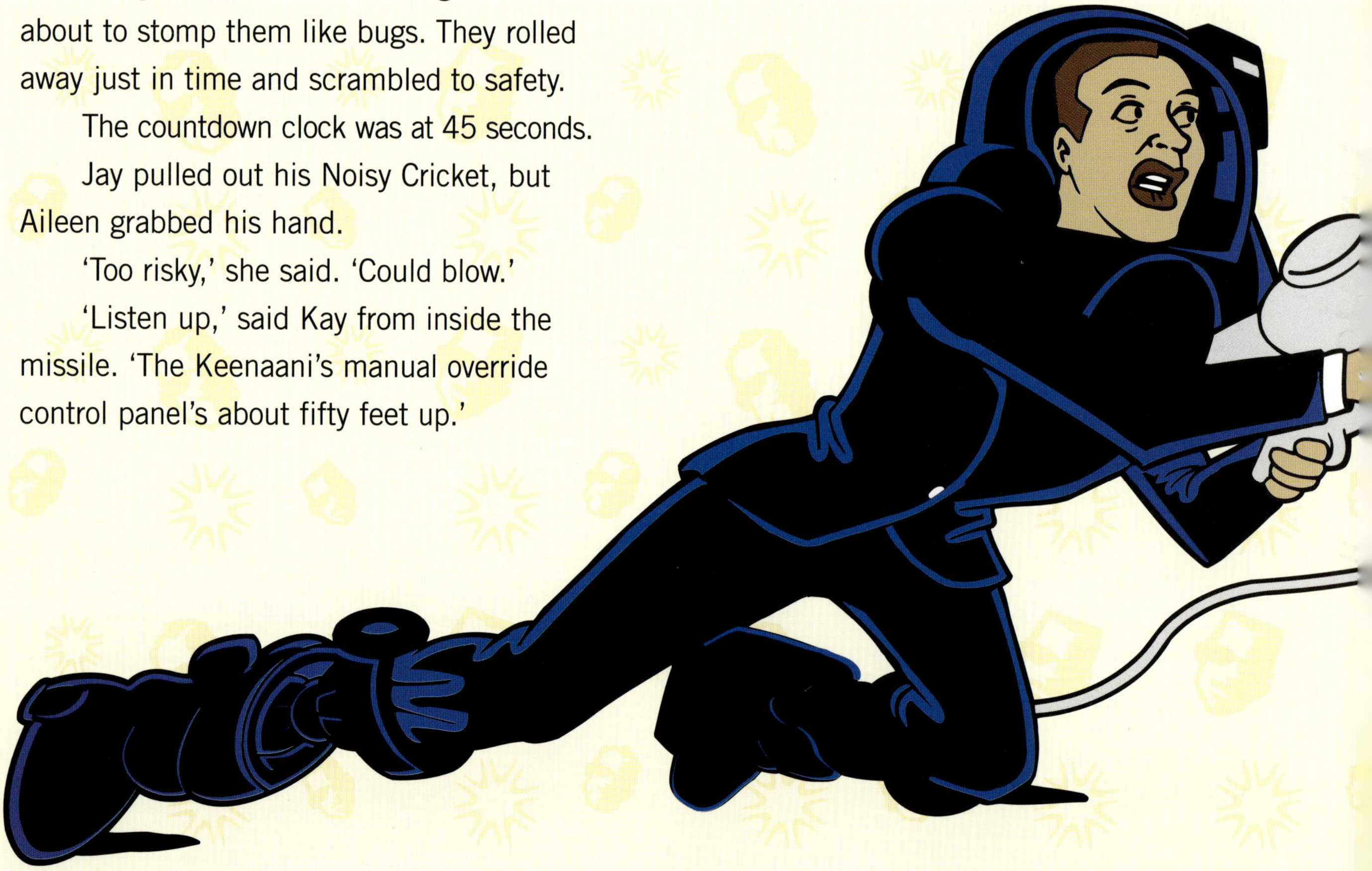

'In position,' he said.

'You've got one shot,' said Kay from inside the missile. 'Enter any code but the correct one and it locks. Guaranteed blast-off.'

'No pressure here,' said a tense Jay.

'The disarm code is two-seven-three-four-five,' said Kay.

Jay was about to enter the code when he stopped. 'No.'

'What??' said Kay.

'In the limo, the speedometer, the radio...they were all messed up, *backwards*. This thing's no good with *numbers*,' said Jay.

'I hope you're right, Slick,' said Kay.

Jay punched in the code 5-4-3-7-2. And the countdown clock stopped with one second to go. Then it flashed: MISSION ABORTED.

The Inanimate knew it had failed – and released its grip on Aileen.

'Nice work boys,' she said, as the Inanimate morphed back to its sponge-and-tentacle form in the blink of an eye. Kay broke free as the Inanimate skittered away.

Aileen and Jay leapt down from the tower, blocking its path. All three agents had their weapons trained on it as it backed into a corner of the silo where there was nothing for it to mimic.

'Nowhere to run, nowhere to hide,' said Jay, coolly.

The Inanimate was defeated.

The Inanimate was loaded into a see-through case on a transport ship, ready for shipment back to Aileen's planet. A few MiB guards watched over the shipment as Kay supervised the loading.

In the Launch Bay Lounge, Elle and Jay looked out the window where Agent U was talking to Zed while holding two Auxy suits and pointing back at Jay.

'Look at it this way,' said Elle. 'You won't be losing Kay – you'll be gaining U.'

Jay approached Kay out on the Launch Bay.

'Kay,' he stammered, 'good luck with Aileen. I mean it.'

'Listen, Slick, I...'

'Don't say anything or I'm not gonna get this out,' said Jay. 'When she's around, you almost smile. You *never* almost smile. Just take it slow...you could crack the face.'

'But I...'

'Read my lips: Aileen's good for you. Now get on that ship and don't look back.'

'Word of advice, sport,' said Kay. 'Stay clear of the ships when they're fuelling. Fumes are affecting your brain.

Jay was confused. 'Aren't you going home with Aileen?'

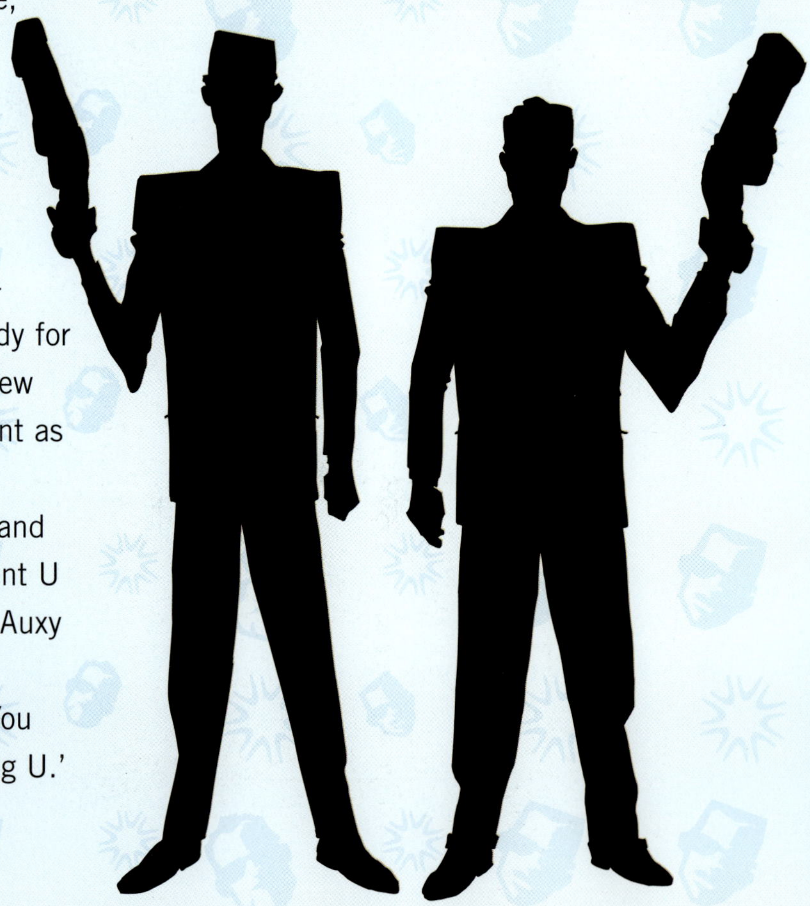

Just then Aileen approached in her true alien form – fiery red cartilage-like dreadlocks, blue translucent skin and those long fingers which entwine to become tentacles. 'Thank for your support, kid,' she said. 'But this really is like old times.'

'I thought you wanted to be...' said Jay.

'We do,' said Kay.

'Just can't agree *where*,' said Aileen.

'Got a hundred cases waiting on our desk,' said Kay.

'And I've got a hundred on mine,' said Aileen.

She turned to Kay. 'Kay...don't be a stranger.'

Kay nodded. 'Small universe,' he said.

Kay and Jay watched as Aileen walked up the ramp of her spaceship.

She paused and called out to Jay. 'And, Slick...take care of our partner.'

Aileen boarded the craft and the ramp retracted. The ship hummed loudly, began to glow with subdued energy and then rose about ten feet, before streaking across the night sky.

Jay looked over to the stone-faced Kay. He was wearing his shades.

'Fuel fumes really sting the eyes, huh,' said Jay.

'Yeah,' said Kay.